THIS BOOK BUILDS ON
A SIMPLE BELIEF: THAT
IT IS MORE IMPORTANT
THAN EVER FOR US TO
GIVE SOME UNDIVIDED
ATTENTION TO THE PEOPLE
WE CARE ABOUT, TO THE
THINGS THAT REALLY
MATTER IN OUR LIVES,
AND TO OURSELVES.

who is this book for, & what does it offer?

It's for people born into a digital world (and for anybody else overwhelmed by its pace and demands) and it offers something we used to take for granted but that we can't take for granted any more:

Uninterrupted time with ourselves, our thoughts, memories, hopes, flights of fantasy, reflections.

It asks us to pause, saying, 'You are going to have a relationship with this book, with this beautiful physical object, which you own, which will challenge you to make it more your own, which will challenge you to write, draw, preserve, resolve, improve and push back against everything the world is asking you constantly to do.'

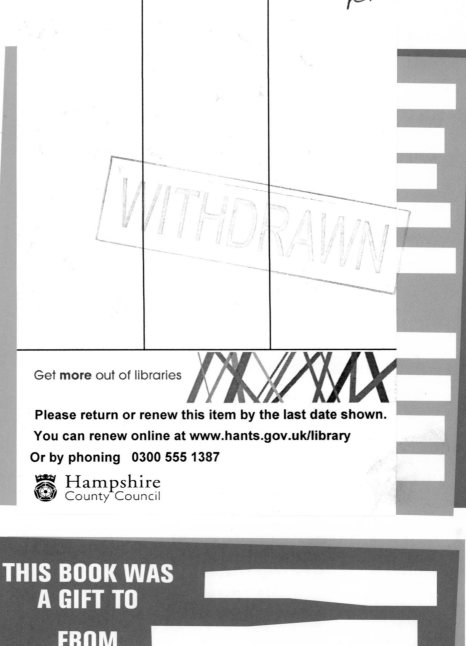

PENGUIN BOOKS

UK | USA | Canada | Ireland | Australia
India | New Zealand | South Africa

Penguin Books is part of the Penguin Random House group of companies whose
addresses can be found at global.penguinrandomhouse.com.

Penguin
Random House
UK

First published 2015
001

Text copyright © Tom Chatfield, 2015

Set in F37 GINGER
Printed in China

A CIP catalogue record for this book is available from the British Library

ISBN: 978-1-405-91936-4

Image credits
Grateful acknowledgement is made by the publisher for
permission to reproduce the images on the following pages:

AKG-Images, Alamy, Gallery Stock, Getty Images,
Mary Evans Picture Library, Shutterstock, Superstock

Claude Lévi-Strauss quote on p.167 © *The Raw and the Cooked* by Claude Lévi-Strauss,
translated by John and Doreen Weightman. Published in 1969 by Jonathan Cape
and reproduced by permission of The Random House Group Ltd.
Andre Gide quote on p.98 © Philosophical Library Inc.
Ernest Hemingway quote on p.154 from *Across the River and into the Trees* by Ernest
Hemingway, published by Jonathan Cape, 1950. Reproduced by permission
of The Random House Group Ltd.

www.greenpenguin.co.uk

MIX
Paper from
responsible sources
FSC
www.fsc.org   FSC® C018179

Penguin Random House is committed to a
sustainable future for our business, our readers
and our planet. This book is made from Forest
Stewardship Council® certified paper.

To buy it is to give yourself a present.

You are going to feel different after using it: more confident, more at home inside your own head.

It's going to help you work out what you really think, want, value and mean.

This book is your invitation to spend some time with the questions that matter most.

Having a thousand messages in your inbox won't make you happy, but carrying this book with you might.

Here, self-expression doesn't mean a tweet, a status update, a performance, and it won't be judged by how many 'likes' you get.

But it is all about making the most of technology as well as your time, becoming a gourmet of the amazing devices and opportunities around you and

Surprising yourself and everyone else by creating ideas, words, responses, relationships and ideals that truly belong to you.

To my wife, Cat, for everything. Again.

To my son, Toby, for coming safely.

To my friend, William de Laszlo, for inspiration.

And to you, of course, for trying this book.

Is there anyone you would
like to dedicate it to?

_____

_____

And any reasons you'd like to give?

_____

_____

_____

_____

OF ALL

how many other things could you be doing right now?

Are email and social media updates lurking in the back of your mind? Do you feel uneasy, relieved — or both — if I suggest that you switch off your phone and set it aside while you sit down with this book?

We live in an age of constant connectivity, and of equally constant anxiety over its consequences. Critics talk about 'digital detox' as though viral videos were akin to fatty foods — and putting our brains on a diet offered a solution to the woes of distraction, attention-depletion and excessive choice.

This book is about something very different. To blame technology is, almost literally, to shoot the messenger. It's like moaning about the fact that we send millions upon millions of emails, text messages and status updates — without stopping to ask why we're quite so keen on sending them.

The answer is, partly, that we love the thrill and validation of what technology offers; that it makes our lives better and richer and easier. But the answer is, also, that we have far less choice or control than it's comfortable to believe. Plenty of people are making plenty of money out of pushing us towards ever-more-frantic online exchange; and plenty of careers, hopes and dreams seem to demand nothing less than a constant show of availability.

here's

HERE'S THE THING

we don't have to accept any of this

This is a book about reclaiming your time. It's also a book for people who love technology; because loving something means using it discerningly, and being able to say not only 'no' and 'yes', but also 'why'?

I love old-fashioned, beautiful books, and I love scrawling my thoughts on to paper. Not because I'm stuck in the past, but because technologies like a pen and paper conjure a time I wouldn't otherwise have.

This is your book, and I hope that the time you spend with it helps you explore questions that go beyond any particular fad or phase. What people, passions, inspirations and ideas deserve your undivided attention? What changes, in your life and the world, do you dream of making in their name?

CONTENTS

LOOKING FORWARD

what if we carried our commitments around with us?

What if we also carried around a lot of other things, caught up in the same pages: memories, surprises, prompts; connections to friends, reminders of what we believe, or what we dream about? You can probably see where I'm going with this.

It has always amazed me how much difference it can make simply to write things down, so that they're there, on paper, looking back from outside of me.

Sometimes, getting ideas and tasks outside of my head is a kind of exorcism, a release of tension. Often, though, it's a gradual process of revelation. I create something – and then I come back to it, again and again, updating and reflecting. I've set myself a standard, and it's my job either to live up to it – or to renegotiate the terms of the deal.

This first section of this book is an invitation to look forward in your life. This doesn't just mean planning things to do. It's an invitation to think about change – what stays the same, what moves on, what you would like to preserve or transform completely if you had the power.

by

By committing things to paper, we give them a life outside ourselves – and we also take a risk. I look back on things I wrote ten years ago, and some of them make me feel sorry or sad. My impulse is to change the words, to say things differently, which is a way of saying that I'd like to go back and speak a few persuasive words to my younger self.

I hope that, in exploring some of the following pages, you have a chance to talk to yourself about change; and to conduct this conversation over a period of time in which you are watching yourself change.

We tend to think of ourselves as a constant, seeing the world through the same eyes from year to year, registering with slight bewilderment the fact that we and everybody else we know are getting older. Yet we alter every day, every moment – even at the core of what we call ourselves. Reading what I wrote ten years ago, writing notes, I find plenty of hope in this.

A rule of thumb for prediction: the longer that something has existed, the longer it is likely to keep on existing. Can you name five things that have existed for over a century that you think will still be around a century from today?

It's unlikely that any of us will be around to see the world in a hundred years' time. If you could see that world, though, what things from today would you most want still to exist?

'THE BEST QUALIFICATION OF A PROPHET IS TO HAVE A GOOD . . .

MEMORY!

GEORGE SAVILE

'NO ONE EVER STEPS IN THE SAME RIVER TWICE, FOR IT'S NOT THE SAME RIVER AND THEY ARE NOT THE SAME PERSON.'

HERACLITUS

Describe a familiar place in a few lines below – somewhere you visit frequently, whether at home, work, or elsewhere.

_____

_____

_____

_____

_____

Record the dates of five further visits below, and next to each record a new observation or thought. Has what you feel about the place changed, or its significance? Has it been changed by others? How does passing time touch it?

1 _____

2 _____

3 _____

4 _____

5 _____

_____

I first encountered this question through the author and cultural thinker Roman Krznaric, and it's a great way of challenging your thinking. If you could do any job in the world for a year, no strings attached, what would it be – and why?

_____

_____

_____

_____

_____

Now consider, what would you most like to change about your own working life – and what would you keep the same? Is it possible for you to do these things? If so, how?

_____

_____

_____

_____

_____

'The brain is a wonderful organ; it starts working the moment you get up in the morning and does not stop until you get into the office.'
Robert Frost

'Good words
are worth much
and cost little.'

George Herbert

Over the next month, try to record here up to
five new words that you've encountered whose
meanings you needed to look up – and write out
your summary of each meaning next to them.

_____

_____

_____

_____

_____

Now take up to five interesting words you
already know and look up their origins, online
or in a dictionary, and write out a summary for
each below: what are the roots of each word?

_____

_____

_____

_____

_____

*Metalexicography - the scholarly discipline of describing
semantic relationships within a language*

Walking between places you already know can offer more new sights than visiting somewhere new. Can you think of two familiar places you would like to walk between – and plan a route connecting them on foot?

Using a map and online tools as needed, write yourself walking directions in the left-hand column opposite. Depending on your experience and fitness, set yourself anything up to a full day of walking.

Mark the crucial turnings, sights and signs you'll see. Carry this book, and try to rely as little as possible on maps, smartphones and other tools. Pack carefully just in case, too: good shoes, layers, water, snacks, cash, phone.

'Perhaps the truth depends on a walk around a lake Wallace Stevens'

Put time aside for walking and plan ahead. Stop somewhere for a meal or picnic, if you like, and watch the world go by. Set yourself free for a day of travel under your own power, soak up the world uninterrupted – and write any notes you like in the right hand column as you walk. What is strange, memorable, makes you look twice; or just a stray thought that rises in your mind?

break your routine

Even small changes can sharpen your awareness of yourself, what you're doing and why you're doing it. Try these five:

Deliberately vary your morning routine: dress in a different order; switch washing, grooming and so on.

TRY DOING THINGS WITH THE OTHER HAND TO THE ONE YOU NORMALLY USE: WRITING, USING A COMPUTER, COOKING.

Instead of texting, emailing and messaging instantly, try composing something fully in your head before you type.

How do you normally greet people? Deliberately use a different phrase or gesture through the day.

How do you hold yourself while walking? Try standing extra-straight, slowing your pace and looking up more.

Did any of the suggestions on the left make you think, or suggest a lasting change you'd like to make? If so, make a note – together with anything else you'd like to try altering.

... A MONSTER WHICH
DEVOURS EVERYTHING;

R'OUTINE.
R'OUTINE.
R'OUTINE.
R'OUTINE.
R'OUTINE.
R'OUTINE.

HONORÉ DE BALZAC

'If by gaining knowledge we destroy our health, we labour for a thing that will be useless in our hands.'

What physical activities do you enjoy most – and why do you enjoy them? Could you spend more time doing them – or get more out of them when you do?

Challenge yourself to think more deeply about the activities you love, and why. Write down up to three that give you pleasure – and what you think are the biggest barriers to doing more of them.

John Locke
LTB30

Try to commit to doing at least one of these activities this month, then another next month, then the last the month after. At the end of each month, write an update; anything significant that has happened, or that you've felt; what, if anything, has changed or could change.

_____

_____

_____

_____

_____

_____

'to others we are not ourselves but performers in their lives cast for a part we do not even know we are playing.' elizabeth bibesco

What was the last live performance you really enjoyed: music, drama; a festival or lecture; circus or spectacle? Whatever it was, however long ago, write briefly below what you remember most vividly – and why it gave you such pleasure.

Are there five live events in the next year that you would really enjoy? Do a little research and make a wish list below, recording what you'd like to attend — and who you'd like to attend with. Write a few notes for each one you've gone to after your visit.

'A serious prophet upon predicting a flood should be the first man to climb a tree.' Stephen Crane

It's easy to be wise after events, but how can we hope to be wise beforehand? The psychologists Gary Klein and Daniel Kahneman suggest this technique. First, set out below your plan for a particular project, or for how you hope an aspect of your life or work will pan out over the next twelve months:

Imagine that it is twelve months from now, and your plan has failed completely. You are conducting a 'post-mortem'. What went wrong? What key weaknesses were revealed?

It sounds odd, but thinking like this can help us uncover the dangers, uncertainties and flaws in our best-made plans and dearest hopes, and then to change our planning by taking account of these.

'YOU ARE NOT ONLY RESPON

BUT ALSO FOR

MARTIN LUTHER

SIBLE FOR WHAT YOU SAY . . .

WHAT YOU DO NOT SAY.'

From promotions and vacations to collaborations and spontaneous acts, if you don't ask, the answer is always 'no'. Can you think of five things it's worth asking for?

1

2

3

4

5

Now that you've got your wish list, try picking your favourite one and answering the questions below (and then acting):

What, exactly, will you ask for?

Who can you ask?

How will you ask them?

When will you ask?

Why should they say 'yes'?

I'm writing these words at half-past nine in the early evening in June in the south of England, looking out from my desk towards the silhouettes of three large trees against a still-bright sky.

I'm always shocked by how deeply my mood and thoughts are shaped by where I am and what I'm doing – and by how little the naked exercise of willpower has to do with any of this.

If I'm sitting at my desk and work is going badly, staring into the intricacy of those trees is a release. But what really changes the way I feel is

getting up, leaving the house and walking out into the world.

I think and I feel differently when I'm in motion. Half a day of walking is the best therapy I know for most of my worst moods. I'm useless at naming birds and trees, but I'm getting a bit better as I practise on the roads and fields near my home; I'm pretty useless at naming local businesses, people and chunks of history, but I'm working at that too.

Looking closely at a familiar place is an everyday kind of magic. But the act of looking itself scratches only the surface of the present.

When I'm walking, it's my steady-stepping body that brings the world to me. My legs loosen as I warm up into movement, my back lengthens and eases; smells tug at memories and feelings before I've noticed their presence. I moved out of London earlier this year, after living there for a decade, and — if I concentrate — the steady sound of birdsong is still a little shocking to ears that barely used to hear it.

In some ways, it's harder than ever for most of us to find the time to look around — and to really see, uninterrupted and unmediated, the places we're in. The gift of constant connectivity easily becomes a curse if we never look up from a screen for long enough to really look at where we are, let alone listen or feel it, or talk to those we're sharing it with.

In other ways, though, we're just as able as ever to change ourselves by letting the world around us in. All we need to do is take a depth breath; and move with our eyes, minds and senses wide open.

'If more of us valued food and cheer and song above hoarded gold, it would be a merrier world.'

j.r.r. tolkien

CLINK! CLINK! CLINK! CLINK!

cheers!

Take the time to savour one piece of food and drink as if you've never tasted it before.

Take a moment to look at it from all angles, then close your eyes and move through each sense in turn.

Smell, touch, listen to the space around you, then finally taste.

Feel the textures. Activate every layer of memory and sensation.

What was your experience like?
What did you feel, think and
associate the experience with?
Describe everything below.

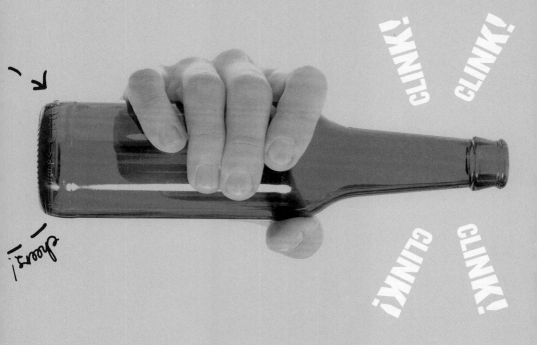

CLINK!
CLINK!
¡CLINK!
CLINK!
¡CLINK!

'NEVER LET THE FUTURE
DISTURB YOU. YOU WILL MEET
IT, IF YOU HAVE TO, WITH THE

_marcus_aurelius_

SAME WEAPONS OF REASON
WHICH TODAY ARM YOU
AGAINST THE PRESENT.'

can you take these 5 21st-century challenges?

1 Don't touch your mobile phone or tablet for a whole day.

2 Walk somewhere you usually drive or take transport to.

3 Start a conversation with a complete stranger.

4 Make a loaf of bread from scratch.

5 Spend an evening at home without electricity: use candles for lighting, a hob or fire for heating. Pretend it's a power cut. Read, talk, play games. Improvize.

If you've succeeded, celebrate!
If not – why not? Write it up.

THEY HAD DONE NOTHING BUT WAIT AND HAD BECOME POETICAL

What do you find the most
beautiful building in your
neighbourhood? Describe
it – and why you love it.
Sketch it below, if you want.

Thomas Hardy

YTO THE SMALLEST BUILDING HOW IMPOSSIBLE TO MOST MEN

What about the ugliest building
near you: can you describe it –
and why it's so different from
the most beautiful building?
Can you illustrate your points?

Make a trip to a place of interest in your local area that you've never visited before: something historical, beautiful, or just unusual. Write up your experience below.

_____

_____

_____

_____

_____

_____

Plan a trip to a place of interest within two hours' travel of where you live. Was it worth the journey? How did it surprise you – or fit in with your expectations?

_____

_____

_____

_____

_____

IT IS GOOD PEOPLE WHO MAKE GOOD PLACES

anna sewell

JEROME
JEROME

'i like work;
it fascinates
me. i can sit
& look at it
for hours.'

K.

JEROME

What are all the different things you spend your time doing during a week? From work to leisure to routine, try listing as many as you can below, in any order, as they occur to you.

Now, try to pick out the three things – however big or small – that give you the most pleasure. And try to explain in a sentence or two why you think they matter to you.

I

II

III

'Hold infinity in the palm of your hand, and eternity in an hour.' **William Blake**

Looking closely at something is a demanding habit. Walk around where you live, slowly, until you find an object you can pick up and feel moved to examine closely. Look at it, handle it, spend a little time with it. Then fill out these notes:

Once you have finished, put the object down – and try sketching it, or part of it, below. Look very closely at its form, its lines. If you look closely enough at just one part, does it start to make the whole seem strange, new, or altered?

I am holding

Against my skin, it feels

It looks like

It reminds me of

I picked it up because

'I'LL TELL YOU HOW

THE SUN ROSE,

A RIBBON

AT A TIME.'

EMILY DICKINSON

What are five of the most common species
of birds and trees near your home? Do
a little research, online or elsewhere,
and write them below.

_____   _____

_____   _____

_____   _____

_____   _____

_____   _____

Now, see if you can also find a short description
of the identifying marks or features of each bird
and the leaf of each tree. Write these below –
and then tick them off one by one once you've
managed to spot a local specimen!

_____

_____

_____

_____

_____

'There is more wisdom in your body than in your deepest philosophies.'

Friedrich Nietzche

Touch is often a neglected sense – and one for which we don't tend to use our whole bodies. Try this exercise to get yourself paying more attention to different kinds of touch.

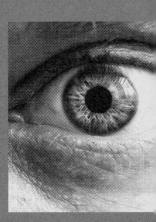

First, get a number of different types of material to create different sensations. Different fabrics can work well: cotton, velvet, lycra; materials like leather and rough paper; small pieces of metal and wood, such as cutlery and pencils.

Now try closing your eyes and touching them against different parts of your body. Not just your hands, but also your cheeks and lips; the crook of your arms and sides; between your toes and behind your knees; brushing them against your hair.

Different parts of our bodies are sensitive in different ways – and convey different kinds of touch, with a different degree of precision and sensitivity.

If you find this interesting, try it with a friend or family member; discuss what you feel; see how quickly you detect a light touch in different areas. How far apart do two different points of contact on your arm or back have to be for you to tell them apart, rather than just register a single pressure?

As you're experimenting with touch, write notes below about the different sensations and points of contact. What is most sensitive, and least? What surprises you the most?

'ANY GLIMPSE INTO THE LIFE OF AN ANIMAL QUICKENS OUR OWN AND MAKES IT SO MUCH THE LARGER

Do you have pets, or contact with many animals? For some people, animals are a huge part of their lives. Others barely consider them. Yet our beliefs about other animals can inform what we think being human means. Try these four questions:

What is your favourite animal?

What are your favourite things about this animal?

What is it about these things you like so much?

Do people share anything in common with this animal?

Now try engaging with an actual animal. If you have pets or close access to other animals, pick one. Otherwise, try to set aside some time to spend with a friend's pet, or an animal in the wild or on a farm that you're able to observe closely. Ask:

What are my feelings about this animal?

What is it that makes me feel these things?

How does the animal itself appear to feel?

How might the world appear to this animal?

HOW LONG IS !T SiNCE YOU LAST?

Told somebody close to you that you love them?

Repaired something with your hands?

Learned a completely new skill?

Told a joke or story that made someone laugh out loud?

What deadline will you set yourself for achieving each of these? Make a note of when you achieve them.

ATTENTION IS THE RAREST AND PUREST FORM OF GENEROSITY

simone weil

CHAPTER THREE

LOOKING BACK

We all tend to impose the stories of our own lives on to the world.

To paraphrase the great British author Douglas Adams:

Anything that was around when we were born is natural and normal; anything invented while we were still young is new and exciting, and anything invented from then onwards marks the end of civilization.

I recently became a father for the first time, and suddenly I find myself looking in from the outside of someone else's childhood. What, I wonder, will my son's generation thank or blame my generation for — if they spend any time doing such thanking and blaming? How will they look back on us?

I was born in 1980, and lived comfortably in the south of England through historical events that shook others' worlds. The fall of the Berlin Wall and the end of the USSR; the end of apartheid in South Africa; the terrorist attacks of 2001 in America; two Gulf Wars. There are 2.5 billion more people alive today than existed when I was born. I will probably live to see 10 billion human beings packed on to our planet. I'm not sure what any of this signifies, but making sense of it is impossible to do alone.

The

The world that feels natural and normal to me was one miraculously altered so far as my grandparents were concerned. And things they once took for granted were already vanishing when I arrived: hats on gentlemen's heads in public places; one pound notes; smoking your way solidly through any kind of journey.

I sit turning the pages of picture books with my son and wonder, will these be the only physical books he ever owns? Does it matter if they are?

This section of the book is about looking back, in several senses: as a journey into memory, into other people's memories, and as a process through which we seek to grasp the world.

Too often, we fail either to celebrate or to learn from the past, such is the speed at which we feel ourselves hurtling into the future. We don't have time for time.

When I look back, I see questions rather than answers, memories I'm testing and remaking, but also something wonderful: the limitless chance to ask, and ask again, what those things I have lived mean.

THAT GREAT CATHEDRA

SPACE WHICH WAS

CHILDHOOD

Virginia Woolf

Write down one of your strongest
childhood memories . . .

_____

_____

_____

_____

_____

. . . and one of your greatest
childhood ambitions or dreams.

_____

_____

_____

_____

_____

'My God, a moment of bliss. Why, isn't that enough for a whole lifetime?'

Fyodor Dostoyevsky

Think of some things you used to enjoy doing when you were younger but which you haven't done for a while.

If you can, pick at least one that you can do or recreate now. Write up your experience below. How did it make you feel?

bliss

'WE SPEND ALL OUR TIME WORRYING ABOUT WHAT WE'RE GOING TO DO, RATHER THAN CELEBRATING WHAT WE'VE ACCOMPLISHED.'
JOHN-PAUL FLINTOFF

Life is full of to-do lists (and so is this book). And
they're great! But you shouldn't forget to keep
the occasional done list too. Write down five
things you're proud you did in the last year . . .

_____

_____

_____

_____

_____

. . . and then five things – anything at all – that
you're proud of having done or accomplished
in the last ten years.

_____

_____

_____

_____

_____

What do you feel are the most significant
historical events that you have lived through
and remember taking place?

_____

_____

_____

_____

_____

What do you feel are the most significant events
that you have experienced yourself (in any way,
even tangentially)?

_____

_____

_____

_____

_____

'LIFE CAN ONLY
BE UNDERSTOOD
BACKWARDS;
BUT IT MUST
BE LIVED
FORWARDS.'

SØREN KIERKEGAARD

'The past is hidden somewhere outside the realm, beyond

Stick, staple or fasten below an object that reminds you
of a recent journey, act or event: perhaps a ticket, a receipt,
a bill, a note, a page, picture, pamphlet, or something else . . .

. . . and return to this one week later, or more, record
the date, and describe below how the particular object
on the left triggers any memories, feelings or thoughts.

THE BEST THING ABOUT THE FUTURE IS THAT IT COMES ONE DAY AT A TIME

ABRAHAM LINCOLN

Imagine that you have a time capsule: a metal box that is going to be buried in the ground and dug up in a hundred years' time by your great-grandchildren. What five objects would you put inside to represent the world as it is today?

Now imagine you are digging up a time capsule that was put in the ground by your great-grandparents one hundred years ago. What objects do you think they might have put in it?

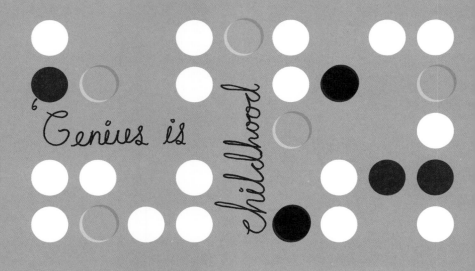

'Genius is childhood

Think of a room that you
remember vividly from when
you were ten years old or less.
Close your eyes – and then try
to list below as many objects
and features as you can recall.
Sketch if you like.

recalled at will.[9] Charles Baudelaire

Now see if you can do the same for a street or outdoor location from the same time in your life. How much detail can you conjure up in your mind's eye and record below? Again, sketch if you like.

Who is the oldest member of your family that you're in contact with — or the oldest close family friend? Take the time to interview them, by phone or in person; ask them to tell you a story from when they were your age, then write out your own short version of it below, in the style of their telling.

_____

_____

_____

_____

_____

_____

Now imagine that you are writing a letter to yourself in the future, when you're the same age as the person you interviewed. Tell your future self in the space below something that has happened recently that you would like to remember, big or small, something you want to preserve.

_____

_____

_____

_____

_____

_____

'Preserve your memories
keep them well

What you

forget you can never retell.'

LOUISA MAY ALCOTT

'NEWS IS WHAT SOMEBODY, SOMEWHERE WANTS TO SUPPRESS; ALL THE REST IS ADVERTISING.'
Lord Northcliffe

In a culture of constant news updates, it can be difficult to take a long-term perspective on events. But that doesn't mean it's impossible to weigh their significance. Try looking through the news today, and outline below what you believe are the five most significant or interesting news stories.

_____

_____

_____

_____

_____

Come back and revisit this page one month after you wrote the list above. For each story you wrote, try to answer these questions: does what happened seem more or less important or exceptional and, in either case, why is this?

_____

_____

_____

_____

_____

_____

_____

_____

_____

_____

'I WENT TO THE WOODS BECAUSE I WISHED TO LIVE DELIBERATELY, TO FRONT ONLY THE ESSENTIAL FACTS OF LIFE . . . AND NOT, WHEN I CAME TO DIE, DISCOVER THAT I HAD NOT LIVED.'

Henry David Thoreau

No matter what your beliefs, death is one of life's few certainties. According to research by palliative care nurse Bronnie Ware, five top regrets recur among dying patients. Try recording a few thoughts in reaction to each of them.

1. I wish I had been true to myself, not others' expectations.

2. I wish I hadn't worked so hard.

3. I wish I'd had the courage to express my feelings.

4. I wish I had stayed in touch with my friends.

5. I wish I had let myself be happier.

Death is often a taboo subject, yet thinking clearly about it can be clarifying and life-enhancing. Now try these five questions.

1. How would knowing you had only a couple of years left to live change your perspective?

2. What would be most important to you in that time?

3. What would you regret doing, and not having done?

4. What might you change?

5. Who would you want to share your remaining time with?

If I close my eyes and try to focus on myself, who exactly is doing the looking — and what are they looking at?

LOOKING

Chapter four

It's not as if there is a place outside myself where I can stand and catch 'me', whole and frozen into a moment. By thinking about my own thoughts, I instantly change them. I can't observe myself in the same way that I look at anything else.

Disciplines like meditation ask us to try losing ourselves; to let go of the insistent 'I' and 'me' that rule our waking moments. I'm never sure that this is either achievable or desirable, but I do think there's something very powerful in the idea of quietening your mind, and letting go of the anxious crowds of everyday thoughts.

The path to this kind of inward looking is almost always rooted in the body, and in calming the senses: deep, steady breathing; relaxed stillness; silence, or rhythmic noise; eyes closed, or gazing at a fixed object. In retreat from the world, we catch glimpses of ourselves in a new light.

This kind of looking is very different from our daily confrontations with images and mirrors. Looking closely at our own bodies is often linked to anxiety, dissatisfaction and pressure. We want to look different – and better! We worry about clothes, passing time, illness, oddness.

In photographs, we see ourselves as if we were strangers: as an image to be preserved, shared, treasured, judged. There's a strange mix of accuracy and exclusion in every one of these images – the perfect reflection of a particular moment that says little about any other moment, what's taking place behind the eyes of its subjects, or what they are surrounded by outside the frame.

This section of the book invites you to look at yourself not simply as the world sees you, but as you appear in moments that catch different aspects of your body, your thinking and feeling, your voice and your touch and your gaze.

We can never know ourselves completely, never hold our-selves still. Yet in looking, listening and recording, we can deepen and celebrate our many parts.

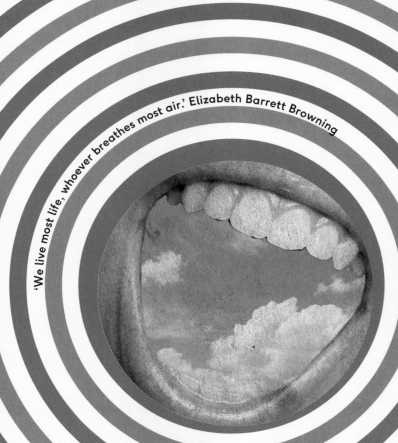

'We live most life, whoever breathes most air.' Elizabeth Barrett Browning

Practise a simple breathing exercise.

Sit somewhere comfortable and quiet, close your eyes, and concentrate on your own breathing in silence.

Don't consciously change your breathing rate, but let the breaths rise and fall naturally.

For one minute, try to empty your mind of any thoughts other than your own breathing.

See if you can manage to take this time once per week — and extend the duration gradually up to five minutes.

What thoughts and feelings rose to the surface of your mind? Revisit this page and scribble your thoughts and impressions.

Sit still, close your eyes and
concentrate on your body.
Scan gently from toes to head.
Where do you feel most relaxed
– and where is the greatest
tension or discomfort?

Go for a brisk walk, and
concentrate on your sensations
as you do so. Is tension being
released, or concentrated in
different areas? How is your
mood? Reflect on your body
in motion.

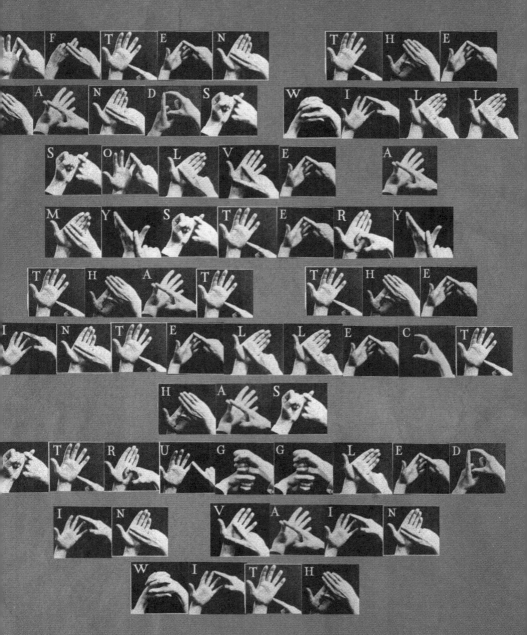

Carl Jung

TRY FILLING IN THE BLANK WORDS BELOW AS THEY OCCUR TO YOU.

I think of myself as a _____ person

who has always loved _____

and would rather _____ than

_____

I can become uncomfortable when _____

_____

and feel most at home when _____

_____

AND THEN COME BACK AT A LATER DATE AND TRY THESE.

My closest friends see me as _____

_____

who is passionate about _____

_____

and prefers _____

to _____

they would say that I dislike
_____
_____

and that I'm at my best when
_____
_____

NEVER TO HEAVEN GO. '

ORDS WITHOUT THOUGHTS

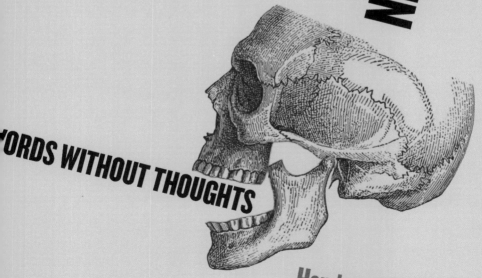

Hamlet, Act III, Scene III

IT IS BETTER
TO BE HATED
FOR WHAT
YOU ARE THAN
TO BE LOVED
FOR WHAT
YOU ARE NOT.
ANDRÉ GIDE

Using your phone, or any other recording device, try speaking into it for thirty seconds in any way you like, beginning, 'Who am I? I am . . .' Play it back and transcribe the result below.

What was it like to listen to and write out your own voice? Did you edit or write exactly what you said? Try the same exercise again, this time starting, 'What do I care about? I love . . .'

Dreams are true while they last, and do we not live in dreams?

Alfred Lord Tennyson

Keep this book beside your bed for a week, and scribble in the space below anything you remember about your dreams when you wake up – however strange or ordinary.

Look back over your notes from time to time, and see whether anything seems to recur: any themes, ideas, people, thoughts. What do they mean to you? How do they make you feel?

Here's a simple exercise that can have a surprising impact. List below any five things that you feel grateful for, big or small.

_____

_____

_____

_____

_____

Now, pick one of them – preferably a day or more after writing your list – and explain below what it means to you.

to be thankful

he man who forgets ∧ has fallen asleep in life

Robert Louis Stevenson

YOU ARE WHEREVER IS MY

Sit, relax, breathe deeply and clear your mind. Imagine: what would a perfect house look like? Not necessarily a realistic or even a possible one, but some perfect place for you to live and thrive. Visualize, wonder, then write or sketch (or both!) your thoughts below.

HOME MY ONLY HOME

CHARLOTTE BRONTË

Read back the description on the left, and now – after a break – try describing below how you might spend a day in your perfect house. What would you do? How would it make you feel? Who or what else might be there with you?

Here's a sensory exercise you can try at home that may seem strange, but that can have powerful results.

What would it be like to lose some or all of the use of one of your senses? You may already know the answer. If not, though, you may find the experiments below interesting.

Try covering your eyes for five minutes – with a blindfold, a piece of cloth or clothing, anything – while you're in a familiar place. Carefully, navigate it by touch and memory.

For touch, try wearing a thick, stiff pair of gloves indoors for five minutes while performing ordinary tasks.

For hearing, wearing a pair of earplugs while going about your daily activities can be a revelation. How does this shift your sense of the world?

For smell, try tasting familiar foods and drink while holding your nose completely blocked. How much of your sensory appreciation is cut off without smell to enhance the taste?

'O for a life
of sensations
rather than
of thoughts!'
John Keats

Once you've tried some or
all of the suggestions on the
left, write below: which sense
would you least like to lose
the use of, and why? What
do you consider most and
least important?

'THERE ARE TWO WAYS TO BE THE CANDLE OR REFLECTS IT.'

Practise your empathy: think of
someone you know well, and
write below a description of
five aspects of their personality
in the first person, as though you
were them: 'I am a . . .'

OF SPREADING LIGHT:
THE MIRROR THAT

EDITH WHARTON

Now try writing five things about yourself, but in the third person, as though writing about yourself from the perspective of the person you described on the left: 'He/she is . . .'

'and you shall know the truth and the truth shall set you free.'

John 8:32

Why be constrained by the way things actually are? Complete the sentences below about yourself in any way you like — but make sure that nothing you write down is actually true.

I am a
_____
_____

I have a talent for
_____
_____

I dream of
_____
_____

My greatest fear is
_____
_____

And I am famous for
_____
_____

Look back over the answers you wrote on the left. What kind of person have you described? Try fleshing out the ideas you've come up with as if they applied to a fictional character – and fill out his or her details below:

This character is a

_____

_____

Who comes from

_____

_____

They learned everything they know in

_____

_____

And they cannot

_____

_____

Although their detractors claim

_____

_____

LOOKING FOR INSPIRATION

I had always loved reading, and always loved writing. From science fiction to selected classics, I lost myself in reading books most evenings. And I wrote most days: stories, poems; notebooks illegibly crawling with ideas; a diary that I stopped keeping after a year because it was so boring when I read it back.

But what I had never done was mixed the two. I never wrote while I was reading. I never even underlined bits I'd enjoyed or wanted to remember. Books were sacred, and writing was separate. Until, one evening, I started having an argument with the book I was reading inside one of its margins.

I started writing notes in the margins of books when I was in my teens, and and it changed my life.

I think it was a novel by Martin Amis, but I can't be sure. What I do remember was the wonderful shock of seeing my own handwriting linked by a thick arrow to the pristine type, spelling out the word 'No!' – followed by an explanation of exactly why I felt that the author was writing rubbish.

Many of my books are thick with notes, today, and I find it hard to imagine reading without a pen in hand – or without highlighting passages of a digital text – or without sharing selected quotations on social media. It has become a way of life, because it's a way of making the experience of reading mine.

It's also a way of holding on to thoughts and hopes that leap into my mind

When

when I'm inspired; of putting my own mind
on to the page so that I can come back later,
remember, disagree, develop and generally
tease out why something matters or means
so much.

Looking for inspiration isn't the same thing as
looking for validation or consensus. You don't
need to agree with something to be inspired.
You don't even to need to agree with yourself,
in the long run.

What you need, I think, is permission to set your
thoughts flowing – and a place to make them
permanent. Write in the margins. Connect your
reactions to the words, images, people, ideas,
sounds, songs, events – anything, everything –
that fuel your most passionate cries of both
'yes' and 'no'!

Write down up to five books
you aim to read this year . . .

_____

_____

_____

_____

_____

. . . and a favourite quote from
each when you've read them.

_____

_____

_____

_____

_____

_____

_____

_____

_____

_____

_____

_____

NOBODY REALIZES THAT SOME PEOPL EXPEND TREMENDOUS ENERGY MERELY BEING NORMAL

ALBERT CAMU

There are some everyday
activities that give us energy
and inspiration; that sharpen
our sense of possibility. What
are five such activities, or ways
of spending time, for you?

_____

_____

_____

_____

_____

There are also things that we
find especially burdensome or
draining; that sap our energy.
What are five of these to you?

_____

_____

_____

_____

_____

List five people you know whose taste
you respect . . .

_____

_____

_____

_____

_____

. . . and ask each of them to recommend a
movie, album or book. Write it below – and try
to watch, listen or read it in the next month.
Afterwards, share your thoughts with them.

'IF YOU HAVE KNOWLEDGE, LET OTHERS LIGHT THEIR CANDLES IN IT.'

Margaret Fuller

‘ (6) best (5) their (7) order;

(4) in (2) is (1) prose (3) words

(16) order. (9) is (15) best (11) best

(12) words (10) the (14) their ,

(13) in (8) poetry

Samuel Taylor Coleridge

You'll find a host of words jumbled below, in
no particular order. Circle your favourite ones
– whatever words, for whatever reason, please
you the most – and underline any you really
don't like . . .

Stately **plump** sustained **aloft** intoned **coarsely** solemnly
mounted gravely **thrice** awaking **gurgling** displeased **coldly**
equine **grained** hued **pale** peeped **smartly** barracks **preachers**
beloved **genuine** soul **corpuscles** rapt **white** glistening **points**
shrill **skipped** shadowed **jowl** patron **absurd** ancient **jest** parapet
lathered dactyls **buck** jejune **ponderous** indigestion **knife-blade**
warily raving **panther** razorblade **perch** scutter **crumpled** sweet
hyperborean kneel **sinister** farther **curled** mummer **jagged** fraying
wax rosewood **wetted** threadbare **sluggish** hollow **poxy** etiquette
paralysis radiant **sombre** lawn **watching** narrowly **dancing** motes

. . . and now write a scene using or inspired
by either (or both!) sets of words.

_____

_____

_____

_____

_____

_____

_____

_____

_____

_____

'Daring
ideas
are like
chessmen
moved
forward.
They may
be beaten,
but they
may start
a winning
game.'

Johann Wolfgang von Goethe

Creativity often begins with brainstorming great ideas – without holding back. Try pouring out below as many ideas as you can come up with, in one minute, for exciting things to achieve during the next week (maximum ten words per idea!).

Creation is also about action, and being selective. Wait a few hours. Now read through your ideas – and pick the two best ones. In as much detail as you can manage, explain below how you will set out to achieve them.

Select ten songs that mean something to you at the moment, write them below, and make them into a playlist for a friend.

1

2

3

4

5

6

7

8

9

10

Now ask your friend to recommend ten songs that they love, write them out below and enjoy both playlists! What does each make you feel? Or seem to have in common?

1

2

3

4

5

6

7

8

9

10

IF I CAN'T DANCE I DON'T WANT TO BE PART OF YOUR REVOLUTION

Emma Goldman
(attrib.)

'FILL YOUR PAPER WITH THE BREATHINGS OF YOUR HEART.' WILLIAM WORDSWORTH

This is an exercise in free writing that you may find easiest to attempt first thing in the morning or last thing at night.

Thinking as little as possible, steadily write down whatever thoughts, images, words, ideas and phrases come into your head in this particular moment.

Anything goes; the more random, spontaneous and disconnected, the better. Fill up the space below in any way you like; don't stop until it's all filled.

Now that you have filled the space on the left with words, revisit it with a critical eye. Try circling any phrases or parts that seem interesting to you – then write them below in a new order and format that pulls them into a whole.

'The poet doesn't invent. He listens.' Jean Cocteau

Below is one of my favourite poems. It's a sonnet, written in 1818 by Percy Bysshe Shelley, called 'Ozymandias'.

I met a traveller from an antique land
Who said: 'Two vast and trunkless legs of stone
Stand in the desert. Near them, on the sand,
Half sunk, a shattered visage lies, whose frown,
And wrinkled lip, and sneer of cold command,
Tell that its sculptor well those passions read
Which yet survive, stamped on these lifeless things,
The hand that mocked them and the heart that fed:
And on the pedestal these words appear:
"My name is Ozymandias, king of kings:
Look on my works, ye Mighty, and despair!"
Nothing beside remains. Round the decay
Of that colossal wreck, boundless and bare
The lone and level sands stretch far away.'

Try reading the poem out loud to yourself, slowly, sounding its rhythms and rhymes. Do you like it? Does it make sense?

Reciting and memorizing poems and lyrics we enjoy can help us make them our own in new ways – can make them a part of us far more than simply listening or reading.

Think of a section of a poem or some lyrics that you love; look them up and write them out below; read them out loud; then try by repetition to remember them, so that you can recite the whole from memory.

What five things most inspire a sense of creativity and possibility in you? This could be people, places, activities; particular locations or moments; food or drink; art or literature, or losing yourself. Anything. What inspires you?

_____

_____

_____

_____

_____

Passion and inspiration are a beginning – but fulfilment usually involves a process of improvement based on reflection as well as repetition, even if you're appreciating others' work rather than creating something yourself.

Try these questions:

What do you consider your most important creative outlet?

Why does it mean so much to you?

What might you do to increase your pleasure in it?

What would be the ultimate experience for you in this area?

Who is a role model for you in deepening your engagement?

'INSPIRATION EXISTS BUT IT HAS TO FIND YOU WORKING.'

PABLO PICASSO

'A PAINTER SHOULD BEGIN EVERY CANVAS WITH A WASH OF BLACK, BECAUSE ALL THINGS IN NATURE ARE DARK EXCEPT WHERE EXPOSED BY THE LIGHT.'

LEONARDO DA VINCI

Pick a painting or work of visual art that you're interested in, look it up online or in a book (or visit it in person) — and try writing about it using the list of questions below as a guide.

Writing about visual art often seems unusual and esoteric, yet it can deepen appreciation without being complex or obscure — as well as helping explore your own reactions and ideas.

Who is the artist, and when were they working?

What is the style and genre of the work?

What materials are used (oil on canvas; pencil on paper)?

How would you describe its colours and textures?

What is happening, or depicted, in the art?

What feature do you find most striking about it?

What other things does it make you think about?

Why might you find yourself reacting in these ways?

LOOKING
TO
OTHERS

CHAPTER
SIX

There's an improvisation exercise in this section that I was taught by my friend Jean-Paul Flintoff (an author I've also quoted elsewhere in the book).

We were due to speak at an event in Amsterdam, and he suggested it to pass the time and get ready. If I'm honest, I had always thought of improvisation as self-indulgent and slightly excruciating. But I let my friend instruct me, and the result was a revelation. You'll find it on pages 146-7.

I felt liberated, stretched in a way I'd never quite experienced, as if I was back in a favourite class at school, learning something new without any preconceptions about how it ought to be useful, or make me more employable, or fit into my expertise.

I've done a few more improvisation exercises since. But the point isn't that I'm especially good at it – I'm not – or that it has become a big part of my life. It's that simply by trusting someone and saying 'yes', I completely changed my attitude towards an area I had dismissed without knowing anything about it.

I don't do this kind of thing nearly as often as I should. I don't think many of us do. Even with people we know well – or think we know well – it can be extremely difficult openly to exchange ideas or skills, without personality or prejudice getting in the way.

To paraphrase another friend who joined in that day in Amsterdam, the author and

psycotherapist

psychotherapist Philippa Perry, in many conversations we aren't really seeing someone else in front of us at all. Instead, we're seeing a ghost from our past; or an image of ourselves; or a pet hate or passion. We think we're looking to others, but we're actually lost in ourselves.

What does it mean to let our guard down, and not only to be our true selves around others, but to be alive to the possibility of extending and improving these selves? The answer is partly about the quality of time and the questions we are able to bring. But it's also about a certain joy and freedom: of letting go without necessarily asking why or what or how.

Other people live in us, and we live through them. Even when we are alone, our hopes and the boundaries of our world are defined by other people.

'Good friends, Good books & a sleepy concience: this is the ideal life.'

Mark Twain

Write down up to five people who deserve some of your quality time, but who you haven't seen or spoken to recently.

_____

_____

_____

_____

_____

Once you've got back in touch (and if it went well!) use the space below to commit to seeing them again: make a plan.

Invite five great people —
friends, family, colleagues
— to share a long, relaxed
conversational meal with
you, at home or out . . .

. . . and write a note afterwards
about what was said, shared
and enjoyed. What memories
do you want to preserve?

Miguel De Cervantes

'EXCELLENCE IS NEVER AN ACCIDENT. IT IS ALWAYS THE RESULT OF HIGH INTENTION, SINCERE EFFORT AND INTELLIGENT EXECUTION.'

ARISTOTLE

Ask five friends this question, and summarize each of their answers — or the best bits of them — below. 'What one new thing would you advise me to start doing to improve my life?'

Now ask the same question to five people you know but don't count as friends, and see what they say. Are there any recommendations you're able or willing to adopt?

I AM SO C

I SO T

SO SOMET I

DON'T UNDER

A SINGLE C

A WORD

EVER HATE TIMES TAND WHAT I AM SAYING

OSCAR
WILDE

Try this improvisation exercise with a friend.

Improvisation often fails if, as in life, there's no tension or animating force beneath its surface.

Decide in advance who is going to be high status – confident, dominating, outgoing, upright and proud – and who is going to be low status – timid, nervous, withdrawn, self-effacing, shy.

Now act out a scenario in which one of you is visiting the other at home. You are old friends, but there is an unspoken issue beneath your conversation that may eventually come out: whoever is higher status has borrowed some money from their lower status friend, and has never paid it back.

Without breaking out of the behaviours appropriate to your status, improvise five minutes of conversation.

Then, if you enjoyed it, try swapping your relative statuses and trying again – or swapping who owes money to whom.

And remember one golden rule. Never reject or negate an idea suggested by your friend. Always accept, build and adapt.

Afterwards, write a few notes on the experience – and on any other scenarios or exercises you might feel like trying!

THE HAPPIEST CONVERSATION IS THAT IN WHICH NOTHING IS DISTINCTLY REMEMBERED

Use the suggestions below as a conversation menu for a meal or drink with friends or family (or interesting strangers). Rather than small talk, pick a starter question per course.

Who did you most admire when growing up, and why?

What are you most afraid of?

What do you love doing for its own sake?

What, for you, does it mean to be successful?

Does it matter what other people think about you?

BUT A GENERAL EFFECT OF PLEASING IMPRESSION

SAMUEL JOHNSON

After you've tried that, write out your own suggestions for a conversation menu below — and try using it with new people. What does it feel like to launch into this kind of talk?

'Children at play are not playing about; their games should be seen as their most serious-minded activity.'
Michel de Montaigne

This is my favourite game for playing with friends and family. You need pencils, paper, a bowl and a timer, plus at least four people, divided into teams of at least two players per team.

Without letting anyone else see, each player writes five names in secret on to five scraps of paper. These should be well-known people or characters that everyone will recognize: living or dead, fictional, mythological, celebrities, anything.

Fold up all the scraps of paper, then mix them in a bowl. Each

round, one person has thirty seconds to pick out papers at random, and to give clues to their team to help them guess the person on the paper. You can pass only once per turn.

In round one, you can say anything you like as a clue, apart from any words written on the paper. In round two, you can use only two words as a clue: any more and it doesn't count. In round three, you can't speak, but must use charades.

Set aside your correct guesses at the end of each turn and switch the performer. When you have gone through every

bit of paper, the round is over; score a point per correct guess.

Repeat for three rounds: highest score wins!

Here's a second game that can be played with two or more players, and which doesn't need any props at all.

The first player names a famous person: living or dead, real or fictional. The only rule is they must give a first and a last name: 'Albert Einstein', not simply 'Einstein', for example.

The next player must then name a second famous person whose first name begins with the same letter as the second name of the previous person.

If the first player says 'Albert Einstein', the second player must then say a name beginning with 'E' — 'Edward Norton', say.

The next player must then follow the same rule, and so on — until someone is stumped. If a player can't think of a new name within ten seconds, they're knocked out.

The only other rule is that if you name a person whose first and last names both begin with the same letter — 'Charlie Chaplin', 'Donald Duck' — play switches direction and goes back to the player who came before the speaker.

Enjoy — and seek out similar new games if you enjoy these.

'TRY TO LOVE THE QUESTIONS THEMSELVES, LIKE LOCKED ROOMS AND LIKE BOOKS WRITTEN IN A FOREIGN LANGUAGE.' RAINER MARIA RILKE

Do you know of someone with an interesting job or hobby, who has had an interesting life, or who you simply find intriguing? Try interviewing them as if you were a journalist writing a portrait. First, decide on five key questions to ask . . .

1

2

3

4

5

. . . and then spend at least fifteen minutes, either in person or via phone, interviewing them. Listen carefully and don't speak too much yourself. What have you learned? Can you summarize their answers to your questions below?

Try practising an exercise in active listening with a friend.

Decide who is going to listen and who is going to talk first.

The talker should speak for three to four minutes about what kind of travel they most enjoy – without mentioning a specific destination.

The listener should focus on actively listening by attending carefully to what is and is not being said, picking up on visual cues, making eye contact and generally presenting an open and encouraging audience to draw out the speaker.

After three or four minutes, the listener should then carefully explain to the talker what they think are the three or four crucial points they've been told – and on this basis they should suggest a potential trip they think the talker would enjoy.

The talker and speaker then spend two minutes together discussing how well they feel they communicated.

After this, swap roles. The core of active listening is the process of one person reflecting back to the other what they think they have heard, and confirming and clarifying together.

ERNEST HEMING WAY

What do you think are the main barriers to understanding fully what someone else means and wants to say?

Are there problems with words; feelings; attention span; distraction; lack of connection; confusion or ambivalence?

Write any thoughts below on what you have found.

'HE THAT HAS ONCE DONE YOU A KINDNESS WILL BE MORE READY TO DO YOU ANOTHER THAN HE WHOM YOU YOURSELF HAVE OBLIGED.'

BENJAMIN FRANKLIN

It can be difficult to ask for help or for a favour
– yet inviting someone to give something or to
share something with you can be both flattering
and a deepening of friendship. Can you think of
five everyday favours you'd like to ask of friends?

_____

_____

_____

_____

_____

And can you now think of five people of whom
you'd like to ask these favours? Note them
below and commit to approaching them
and noting the result (and thanking them
afterwards). Gratefully accepting a gift
is a talent as significant as giving well.

_____

_____

_____

_____

_____

_____

_____

_____

This is an exercise often recommended to people with difficult lives, but one that can be revealing for anyone. It's about looking at the people in your life, and seeing where you give and receive support.

Write your own name near the centre of these two pages, then write the names of important people in your life around you: friends, family, colleagues. Draw an arrow from each person towards you if they are someone from whom you feel you receive support. If you get a lot of support, make it a strong, thick arrow; if you get a little, make it smaller and thinner.

Once you've done this, try putting in a second set of arrows pointing away from you and towards the people to whom you feel you give support. You may well need to write in new names on the page. The arrows can bend as much as you like – again, make their size in proportion to the level of support.

What does the diagram suggest about your life? Are you receiving as much support as you give? Which relationships are balanced between give and take? Which go one way?

If you're going
through hell,
keep going.

Winston
Churchill

LOOKING TO MAKE A DIFF

CHAPTER 7

ience

Where to start if you want to change the world? Most of us care most deeply about people and events we're close to: our neighbourhood, our family, problems that directly affect our own lives. But this doesn't mean we believe we can change things.

When causes or consequences are distant from us in time or space, we tend to feel less responsible, or less obliged, or less able to understand what's going on (or all three at the same time). This is understandable. But it's also a big problem for all of us when it comes to the world's greatest challenges.

If I dropped some litter outside your house, you might shout at me to pick it up. But neither of us would expect me to pick up other litter off the pavement as I walked along. If neither of us saw it happen, it's not our problem. Even though filthy local pavements may actually be more of a problem for both of us than any individual littering.

It's easy to dismiss most of what happens outside our immediate experience or expertise as someone else's problem. And yet, for all of us, there are things we either wish to see preserved or changed in the world; and both of these possibilities demand our attention.

Almost everything we value — freedom, security, opportunity, nature itself — can be damaged or destroyed, if enough people allow it to be. And while this sounds like a gloomy thought, it's also a fact that brings a hopeful recommendation. Everything and anything we do can make a difference, if we're prepared to ask carefully enough what kind of a difference we want to make.

This part of the book is about what you think matters — and why it's worth defending. It's about what you admire in other people, and how their achievements may apply to you. It's also, above all, about why the idea of 'making a difference' isn't just a dead phrase hovering around acts of charity. It's a principle for living that can enrich every day, if you let it.

A confession: I don't give away nearly as much of my time, money or attention as I ought to. Few of us do. But being demoralized is worse than useless. Instead, gradually, falteringly, I try to do a little better.

WHEN IT COMES TO THE PINCH HUMAN BEINGS ARE HEROIC

GEORGE ORWELL

List five of your personal heroes below – in any field, in any order – and one thing about them you admire . . .

————————————————

————————————————

————————————————

————————————————

————————————————

. . . and then try to research one new thing that you didn't already know about each of them, and write it below.

————————————————

————————————————

————————————————

————————————————

————————————————

————————————————

————————————————

————————————————

————————————————

Take something that you know how to do or understand – whether it's making a perfect cup of coffee, picking the right clothing for work, or how the tides work – and write out below a brief, clear explanation encapsulating your knowledge.

Now ask someone you know to explain anything new to you that they understand and you do not, then write out below a clear summary of what you've learned from them.

The scientific mind does not so much provide the right answers as ask the right questions.

Claude Levi-Strauss

'I WOULD MAINTAIN THAT THANKS ARE THE HIGHEST FORM OF THOUGHT, AND THAT GRATITUDE IS **HAPPINESS** DOUBLED BY **WONDER.'**

G. K. CHESTERTON

Write with personal thanks to five people who have done or created something you admire or enjoy. This could be an author, musician, organization, artist, politician, anyone! Send a letter, email or card, and explain why you're grateful.

Has anyone acknowledged your message? If they have, note who it was below – together with anything specific they've said to you in return that you wish to remember and preserve.

'THE GR
SERVIC
CAN BE R
ANY CO
TO ADD
PLAN
ITS CU

EATEST
WHICH
ENDERED
NTRY IS
USEFUL
T TO
TURE'

THOMAS JEFFERSON

Growing something at home and then eating it can offer a whole new perspective on food and the rhythms of living.

Try it — even if it's just a few herbs on a windowsill, you can brighten up a meal, and experience a different kind of time to daily and weekly shopping as you wait for your crop.

In the summer, growing mixed salad leaves from seed in a pot or flower bed gives results in a month or even less. Mint is also an incredibly vigorous, robust herb that almost grows itself.

Bulbs like onion and garlic can be planted in spring or autumn — if the soil is well drained, simply wait for them to grow.

Small bushes of cherry tomatoes also grow brilliantly in pots and window boxes — and fast. Feed and water them, growing them either from seed or small pre-planted 'plug plants'.

If you prefer fruit, try buying a lemon tree in a pot. It's not the cheapest purchase: but if you water it and buy lemon food to keep it healthy, a tree placed in a warm, light indoor spot will give fruit you can pluck and use whenever you like.

Once you've experimented with even a little home-growing, try to share what you've done.

Give some of your home-grown crop to friends and family, and offer them seeds and cuttings too, so that they can grow their own in turn.

Finally, keep a record below of what you've sown, harvested, shared and eaten: scribble some notes below celebrating when, where and how you've gone from earth to table.

'IF WE EXTEND UNLIMITED TOLERANCE EVEN TO THOSE WHO ARE INTOLERANT ... THEN THE TOLERANT WILL BE DESTROYED, AND TOLERANCE WITH THEM.'

KARL POPPER

Think of an idea, political
position or principle that
you believe in and think is
important. Try to outline your
beliefs below, explaining why
you believe them to be correct.

Now see if you can outline,
below, what you think of as the
strongest possible argument
against your position. What are
the most compelling objections
anyone could put to you?

'DON'T TELL ME TH[
SHOW ME THE G[
BROKEN GLASS.

A classic rule of writing is 'show, don't tell' —
using detail to engage an audience's senses
and conjure a sense of life. Try experimenting
below with 'showing' for each situation:

Don't tell me it's cold; show me

Don't tell me he was tired; show me

Don't tell me she was cruel; show me

Don't tell me it was amazing; show me

Don't tell me they were afraid; show me

MOON IS SHINING;
NT OF LIGHT ON
ANTON CHEKHOV

Showing is true of life as well as art: actions show faith and determination where words are only abstract. Try completing the sentences below as advice for decisive, specific actions. As with good writing, the more concrete and vivid, the better!

Show you're kind by

Show you're happy by

Show you're grateful by

Show you're welcoming by

Show you're generous by

'IF YOU WANT TO BUILD A SHIP, DON'T DRUM UP THE MEN TO GATHER WOOD, DIVIDE THE WORK AND GIVE ORDERS. INSTEAD, TEACH THEM TO YEARN FOR THE VAST AND ENDLESS SEA.'

ANTOINE DE SAINT-EXUPÉRY

With online resources at most fingertips, learning new skills is easier than ever, but choosing something and sticking with it is tough. List below one new skill that you would like to acquire this year — and four resources that will help you.

_____

_____

_____

_____

_____

Teaching yourself something takes dedication, but you can learn just as much by teaching someone else. List below one skill that you are able to teach someone else, the resources you can use and someone you're willing to start teaching.

'IT IS MORE DIFFICU AWAY INTELLIGENTL THE FIRST PLACE.'

Volunteering to give your time and skills can be remarkably easy – and rewarding. It works best if you pick something achievable that you care about and enjoy.

Can you list below five forms of volunteering you could contribute towards in your local area – and then pick which you'll try giving just a couple of hours a week to?

T TO GIVE MONEY THAN TO EARN IT IN

ANDREW CARNEGIE

Making a donation to charity, however small, can transform others' lives. One source of inspiration is philosopher Peter Singer's book and website *The Life You Can Save*, which publishes a regularly updated list of ten charities judged to be the best at turning your donation into benefit for others.

Try looking it up, finding a cause you believe in – there or elsewhere – and recording and celebrating your giving below.

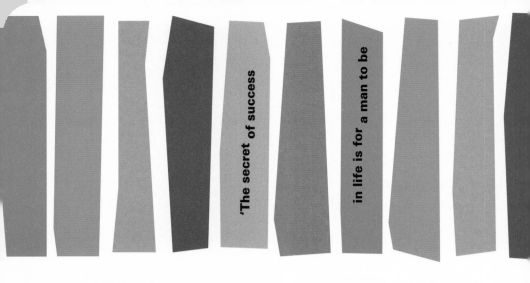

'The secret of success in life is for a man to be

What kind of practical projects are you passionate about? If you could found any business, charity, factory, company or organization, what would it make or do? If you were guaranteed support, what five projects might you begin?

_____

_____

_____

_____

_____

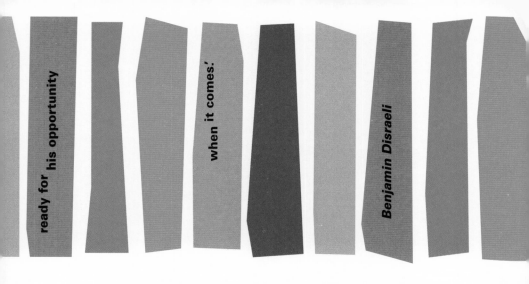

'ready for his opportunity when it comes.'

Benjamin Disraeli

Pick your favourite idea from the left and try
to answer the questions below for it. Pretend
you're trying to persuade someone to back you.
Do you find your answers convincing?

What problem are you solving?

Who wants what you're offering?

Who else does what you're doing?

What will you do better than them?

Why should I help and support you?

"DEMOCRACY CANNOT SUCCEED UNLESS THOSE WHO EXPRESS THEIR CHOICE ARE PREPARED TO CHOOSE WISELY."

FRANKLIN D. ROOSEVELT

Some people think about politics every day; others almost never. Yet almost every aspect of life is touched by political questions. What do you think are the three most important political issues in your country at the moment?

1

2

3

Try summarizing your own opinion about each of these issues in one or two sentences: what you think ought to be done, or valued, or considered most important for each? Are your beliefs reflected by those in power? If not, what are the alternatives that better reflect what you think is right?

1

2

3

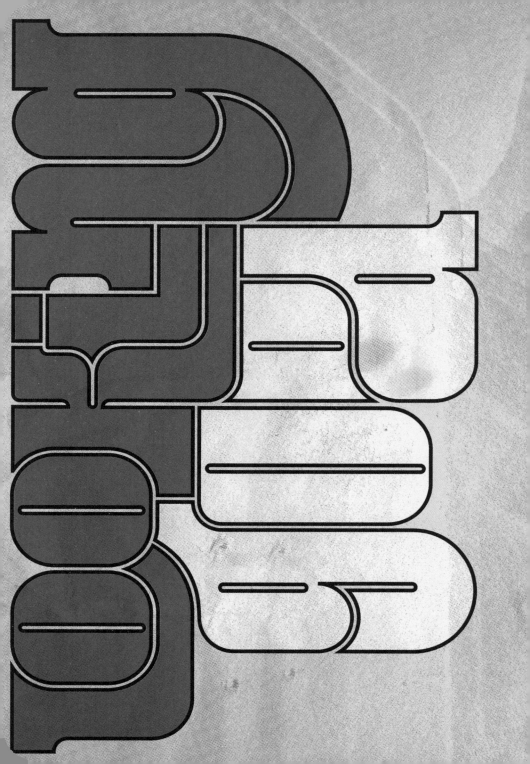

chapter 8

When I was young, I wasn't much good at sports. I was quite shy, I was physically awkward, I wore extremely thick glasses. I could never work out how some children managed to be so relaxed inside their own skins. It seemed an astounding accomplishment: not confidence, but ease. They looked good by looking like they weren't even trying.

Over the years, I've tried very hard to look like I'm not trying when I do some things: public speaking, performing music, meeting new people. I've discovered that I rather enjoy public performance — but that I still feel like a nervous nine-year-old when I make small talk with new people.

What I have managed to do, however, is become more comfortable with my own discomfort. It hasn't vanished; it just doesn't bother me as much. I've got to know myself better. And this includes a certain amount of mumbling and fiddling with glasses.

There are other things I've done, too, of course. I've tried to exercise and increase my physical confidence; I've tried to get better at resting and relaxing; I've tried to put myself in new situations, and to find ways of enjoying them (anticipation is always the worst bit). I've pushed myself to do the things I want to do as well as I can – and I'm still pushing, because there's a long way to go.

In fact, I'm not sure there's a final destination at all. When you use a phrase like 'looking good', it often sounds like you're entering some kind of competition: that it's about being the most stunning person in a room, commanding everyone's attention, sweeping strangers off their feet, and so on.

To me, though, what it actually means is getting better at being yourself. There's no perfect end point – and no first prize. There's just your ability to feel more comfortable more often, more prepared and engaged, and genuinely happier to meet others and do the things you want to do.

If you want to improve yourself, that's great! Learn another language, acquire new skills, hone your talents. But don't forget simply to cut yourself some slack, smile and enjoy looking exactly the way you already do.

A DIFFERENCE OF TASTE IN JOKES IS A GREAT STRAIN ON THE AFFECTIONS

GEORGE ELIOT

Can you collect five funny one-liners over the
next month?

_____

_____

_____

_____

_____

And what's the funniest story you've ever heard?

John
Lubbock

RESTLESSNESS

Our mind needs rest and recuperation every bit as much as our bodies. But mental rest isn't just emptiness; it can also be the freedom of something private yet entirely absorbing.

Write down five activities that occupy your whole attention . . .

_____

_____

_____

_____

_____

. . . and once you have made the time to do one (or some, or all) of them, how did you feel afterwards?

'The limits of my language mean the limits of my world.'

Ludwig Wittgenstein

Below is a list of the ten most common nouns in English. Pick a foreign language you don't know very well, but might like to learn, and look up and write down the translation for each.

1 Time

2 Person

3 Year

4 Way

5 Day

6 Thing

7 Man

8 World

9 Life

10 Hand

Now try translating these further lists of verbs, adjectives and prepositions – plus the numbers one to ten if you fancy – and see if you can memorize them over the next month. It's amazing how much a few key words allows you to understand.

One	To be	Good	Of
Two	To have	New	In
Three	To do	First	To
Four	To say	Last	For
Five	To get	Long	With
Six	To make	Great	On
Seven	To go	Little	At
Eight	To know	Own	From
Nine	To take	Other	By
Ten	To see	Old	About

There's a difference between important and urgent tasks. Urgent things need to be done right now, but in the long term, it's accomplishing important things that really matters. Write below up to five tasks you feel are truly important to you.

_____

_____

_____

_____

_____

Now that you've decided on some important tasks, try this technique for focusing on one thing you want to achieve.

It's called the Pomodoro Technique, after the Italian for 'tomato', because its creator – Francesco Cirillo – based it on using a kitchen timer that looks like a tomato!

Having decided what task you're going to focus on, set a timer for twenty-five minutes. Put the timer in front of you, and work on the task with complete focus and no interruptions for that time. If you can, try using a physical kitchen timer for the above rather than your phone. It's all about eliminating distractions.

When the twenty-five minutes are up, take a five-minute break. Do something – anything – completely different. Or nothing at all.

You've completed one Pomodoro! Set the timer for another twenty-five, followed by another five-minute break, then do another.

If you've managed four in a row, take a thirty-minute break.

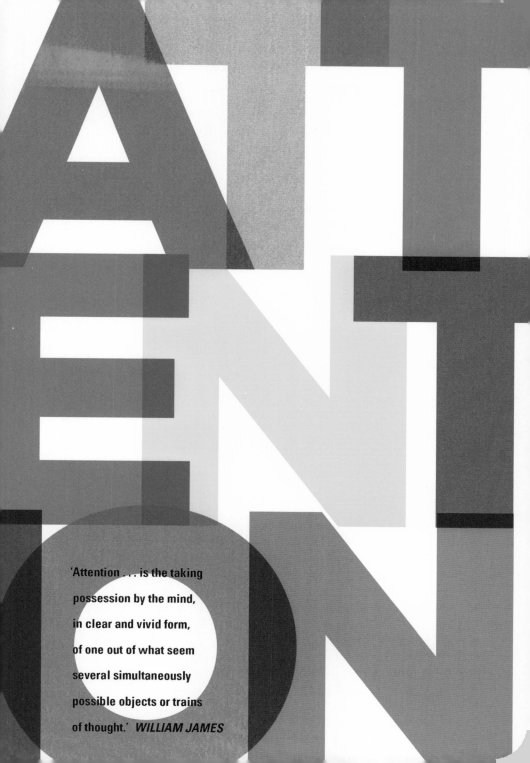

'Attention . . . is the taking possession by the mind, in clear and vivid form, of one out of what seem several simultaneously possible objects or trains of thought.' *WILLIAM JAMES*

'TELL ME WHAT

YOU EAT,

AND I WILL
TELL YOU,

WHAT YOU ARE

JEAN ANTHELME
BRILLAT-SAVARIN

Look up a recipe for a cheap,
tasty dish and write it out
below (if you cook a lot, try
to search out something new).
Try to choose something
fairly simple that you will
enjoy eating.

Now that you have your recipe,
cook it and eat it a few times.
Each time you do, record below
how well it worked, and any
notes or improvements for
next time.

*'The abitily to simplify
means to eliminate
the unnecessary so that
the necessary may speak.'*

Hans Hoffman

When, where and with whom
do you feel you're at your best?

My best time of day is . . .

My best time of the year is . . .

When it comes to company, I'm at my best . . .

With places, I'm at my best in . . .

I think my best thoughts when . . .

'The best cure for

Do you get enough good-quality sleep? The list below suggests ten factors that help with a good night's sleep. Mark for each whether it does (tick) or doesn't (cross) apply for you.

An approximately fixed time for going to bed.

An approximately fixed time for waking up.

No alcohol in the four hours before sleep.

No caffeine in the four hours before sleep.

No heavy eating in the four hours before sleep.

Regular daytime exercise (but not right before bed).

Clean, comfortable bed and bedding.

Quiet, peaceful room for sleeping.

Bedroom at a comfortable temperature.

A peaceful bedtime routine without excess stimulation.

insomnia is to get a lot of sleep.'

The list on the left isn't infallible or exhaustive — especially if you have young children — but if you have more crosses than ticks, you may want to try making some changes. Write below what you might change, and how; or, if you sleep well, what you feel is most important to preserving your good sleep.

W. C. Fields

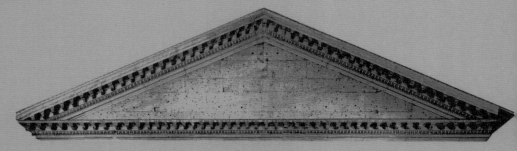

'We do not know the true value of our moments until they have undergone the test of memory.'
Georges Duhamel

One of the oldest techiques around for building a well-stocked mind is known as the 'memory palace'.

Used by the ancient Greeks and Romans, you begin by visualizing in your mind a detailed place within which to 'keep' your memories. This can be an imaginary building, but you may find it easier to use the different rooms of a real building you know extremely well – your home, for example.

Once you have a clear vision of this place in your mind, you now need to turn all the things you wish to remember into a series of distinctive physical objects to put in your 'palace'.

Let's say you are trying to remember a sequence of playing cards. The eight of hearts might become a giant snake curled into the shape of an eight, wrapped around a crimson heart; the two of clubs two giant, crossed metal clubs; and so on.

Once you have come up with a vivid image for each object or idea, you then imagine walking on a journey through your palace, putting the objects in sequence in different places.

When you need to remember, you simply journey once again through the palace in your mind, visiting the objects in turn.

Try the technique yourself! Write a list of ten or more objects below, and see if you can fix vivid versions of them around a suitable 'palace'. Later on, you can also try putting representations of documents, art, books and ideas into it, or making it the permanent host of important memories.

Do you enjoy public speaking? Even for experienced speakers, watching yourself talk can be revealing. Using a phone or similar device, record a video of yourself speaking for five minutes on one of the topics below:

When I want to relax, I

When I was ten years old, I wanted to

My favourite kind of music is

The most important lesson I've learned is

Here are my instructions for making the perfect

Watch the video of yourself all the way through. How do you look and what you're saying come across as you expected?

Imagine you are a public-speaking coach: were you speaking slowly, clearly and engagingly? Did you look at the camera, have good body language and perform confidently? What advice would you give yourself in order to improve? Write your five best tips below, then try again with another topic!

"THE SECRET
OF SUCCESS
IS SINCERITY.
ONCE YOU CAN
FAKE THAT
YOU'VE GOT
IT MADE."

JEAN GIRAUDOUX

It is quite an art both to receive a compliment well, and to offer a compliment sincerely. Both are worth practising! Imagine that someone has just congratulated you on 'doing a truly superb job'. Try writing five gracious replies below that don't shrug it off (don't just claim 'it was nothing . . .'):

Now try writing five everyday compliments that you might comfortably be able to offer to people you encounter on a daily basis: not too excessive, specific rather than vague, and above all sincerely meant and considered. Have a go:

'IN VAIN HAVE
I STRUGGLED.
IT WILL NOT
DO. MY FEELINGS
WILL NOT BE
REPRESSED. YOU
MUST ALLOW
ME TO TELL
YOU HOW
ARDENTLY
I ADMIRE AND
LOVE YOU.'

JANE AUSTEN

We don't consciously think about most of the things we do every day. We'd go mad if we did. Imagine if you had to think carefully about every single movement made by your fingers, every step your legs took, every mouthful of food and sip of a drink, every glance and gesture, every factor in every decision.

Even when it comes to big decisions – what car to drive, what phone to buy, what job to take – we think hard about something once, then tend to stop thinking about it after it's done. We make a conscious choice, once; then our choice vanishes beneath our attention and becomes just another routine.

There's nothing wrong with being creatures of habit. At the same time, it's incredibly unlikely that we're already doing everything in the best way possible, or that all our past decisions were perfect. The question is: how can we identify and improve a few areas in our lives without getting completely lost?

This section of the book is about looking again at ourselves, our habits and our assumptions. As you may notice, I'm especially interested in habits linked to technology. Not because these are the most important of all, but because they can be easy to challenge and change – and because they can suggest all kinds of other changes in turn. Even something as simple as altering how often you check your email can have a big impact (briefly: less is more).

What is a habit in the first place? It's probably something you do regularly, and without much thought, but there's no strict definition. Our habits define who we are – and we may be extremely reluctant to get rid of some of them, even if we can't explain what particular good they serve.

This makes perfect sense. Life is about more than efficiency, and not all habits are bad. Looking again at those things we do without thinking doesn't mean we have to change them: it may simply give us a deeper appreciation of who we are.

I almost certainly shouldn't drink so much coffee; I ought to spend less time playing video games. For now, though, I'm content to be a person who does these things, and whose better battles lie elsewhere.

What do you think are five of your very best habits? What do you do regularly that you're proud of? Celebrate them below.

Why do you think the habits on the left are positive? What is it they give you? For each good habit, try listing what it is about your personality or identity that you feel is reinforced.

_____ _____

_____ _____

_____ _____

_____ _____

_____ _____

THE POWER OF HABIT AND THE CHARM OF NOVELTY ARE THE TWO ADVERSE FORCES WHICH EXPLAIN THE FOLLIES OF MANKIND

Maria De Beausacq

Write down five things in your life that
technology enables and enhances . . .

_____

_____

_____

_____

_____

. . . and five things that you're best able
to do, feel or achieve when you're
unplugged from technology.

_____

_____

_____

_____

_____

'The question of whether computers can think is just like
the question of whether submarines can swim.' Edsger W. Dijkstra

I PREFER
DRAWING
TO TALKING.
DRAWING IS
FASTER AND
LEAVES
LESS ROOM
FOR LIES.

Le Corbusier

Draw a favourite place, or
a person you know well, below
— from memory, in any style
you like.

And now draw a place or
person from life, sitting and
watching as closely as possible
for as long as you're drawing.

Below are ten common clichés:
ways of expressing an idea that
require no thought, that lack
precision, and that over-familiarity
makes almost invisible. Read
them closely . . .

At the end of the day . . .

Taking the path of least resistance . . .

Last but not least . . .

To add insult to injury . . .

It's a blessing in disguise . . .

It was a breath of fresh air . . .

A fate worse than death . . .

Keeping your head above water . . .

There was method in her madness . . .

Time to put your money where your mouth is . . .

. . . and see if, for each one, you
can come up with your own fresher
and more interesting way of making
the same point.

'...avoid clichés like the plague. Always add hat.' anon.

BILL GATES

'I RECEIVE A TON OF SPAM EVERY DAY. MUCH OF IT OFFERS TO HELP ME GET OUT OF DEBT OR GET RICH QUICK. IT WOULD BE FUNNY IF IT WEREN'T SO IRRITATING.'

Email can be both overwhelming and trivial. But you can push back. Carefully compose in this space a message that you've really thought about, for someone who really matters. Then type it out and send it to them.

If they reply, are their words worth preserving? Are there other onscreen words that deserve permanence? Pick a few of the best, most interesting, wisest or simply amusing digital messages you've encountered – email, status updates, tweets, texts – and write them out below.

here is only one

corner of the

universe you can be

certain of improving,

and that's your own

self.' Aldous Huxley

Take a selfie on your phone or camera – or get someone else to take a photo of you. Look carefully at the image and write a description of yourself in it as if you were a stranger . . .

. . . and now try putting away
the image of yourself, and
instead sketching a face,
figure or scene below that
corresponds to the description
you've written on the left.

Do you have any time-wasting habits that you wish you didn't indulge quite so often? List any that you can below – and try to estimate alongside how much time they take up each week.

Pick whichever one takes up most time, and see if you can track it for a week below, recording at the end of each day approximately how much time it took up. Can you cut down?

'I WASTED TIME, AND NOW DOTH TIME WASTE ME.'

RICHARD III

ACT V, SCENE V

OWN WHAT
ONLY WHAT
YOU CAN ALWAYS
CARRY WITH YOU:
KNOW LANGUAGES
KNOW COUNTRIES
KNOW PEOPLE
LET YOUR MEMORY
BE YOUR
TRAVEL
BAG.

Aleksandr
Solzhenitsyn

Think of a foreign country that you don't know much about, one you're intrigued by. See if you can answer the following questions by researching them, online or elsewhere.

What's the biggest news story
there at the moment?

Who is a great national hero,
and why?

What happens in a famous book
written by a local author?

Which countries have been at war
with this one? Why?

What might people there eat
for breakfast?

Now imagine that you're explaining your own country to someone visiting from the country above. How might you answer these questions if they asked you?

What are people most worried
about at the moment?

Where are the most beautiful
places to visit?

What should I eat here if I want
a good, typical meal?

What things do you do best in
your country?

How has life changed here during
your lifetime?

Thinking hard about language can enrich your relationship with the world. Try completing the metaphors below in any way that feels interesting, striking, witty or beautiful.

1 As rough as

2 As dark as

3 Running like

4 As rich as

5 As busy as

6 As lonely as

7 As happy as

8 As noisy as

9 As angry as

10 As thoughtful as

Now try mixing up the suggestions you've written by applying them to other phrases. If you wrote 'As rough as X', write it below instead as 'As rich as X', and so on. Switch your metaphors around, then circle the best and most memorable.

1

2

3

4

5

6

7

8

9

10

'Though analogy is often misleading

it is the least misleading thing we have.'

Samuel Butler

I WOULD NEVER DIE FOR MY BELIEFS BECAUSE I MIGHT BE WRONG

BERTRAND RUSSELL

Our beliefs about other people's beliefs are powerful things – but they're often far from accurate. Complete these statements by inserting two brief descriptive phrases.

In conversation, other people tend to think that I'm _____ and _____

Other people's first impressions of me are _____ and _____

When someone gets to know me, they learn that I'm _____ and

To people working alongside me, I come across as _____ and _____

Ask my friends about the two things I do best, and they'd say _____ and _____

And now try putting the questions below to someone who knows you well – either a friend, family member, colleague, or anyone else. How do their answers compare to yours?

In conversation, you come across as _____ and

My first impressions of you were that you were _____ and _____

As I got to know you, I learned that you are _____ and _____

I'd say that, to those working with you, you come across as _____ and

Two of the things that you do best, in my opinion, are _____ and _____

STOPPING LOOKING

STOPPING LOOKING

CHAPTER 10

IF YOU SPEND YOUR ENTIRE LIFE LOOKING FOR SOMETHING

you're likely to end up disappointed. And while disappointment has its advantages as a source of motivation, perhaps its greatest disadvantage is that it stops you appreciating what you already have.

What do you have to be grateful for? Life itself is a remarkable one-off: a glittering universal exception against a background of near-infinite non-existence. As the saying goes, you're dead a long time.

If you think this sounds bleak, think again. No matter what your spiritual beliefs – or lack of them – the world as we know it is a once-only proposition, and a dazzling one at that. There is pain, loss and tremendous unfairness. But there is also gratitude, love and human possibility, for as long as there are people to experience and deserve these things.

Most of our anxieties tend to reflect things we do not control: future accidents and dangers; random losses or bad luck; our best hopes not working out. For many ancient Greek

philosophers 231

philosophers, accepting the fact that we control almost nothing in our lives was seen as the first step towards wisdom. Only when you've accepted that you personally have very little influence on the future, they argued, can you begin to achieve an accurate perspective on life.

I think they were right to say this. And yet, of course, I myself worry desperately about the future: about harm coming to the people and things I love; about the world, injustice, fate, human foolishness; about absurd appalling possibilities that refuse to leave my head late at night

This doesn't mean I take no comfort from philosophy, or from trying to get things in perspective. In fact, I relish it precisely because of my ongoing wrestling match with anxieties, ambitions, self-obsession and everything else muddying the waters of my existence.

I have a lot I want to appreciate. I don't want to waste my time on stuff that doesn't matter. I want to control the only thing I can even hope to control: myself. And so I hope this final section helps you do the same: to think about changes that might simplify your life, clarify your priorities and help you cherish the joys lurking right underneath your nose.

'YOU HAVE POWER OUTSIDE EVENTS. RE WILL FIND STRENGTH

Can you list below five things that worry you – and note for each whether you feel you do or don't control them?

For those you don't control, try to write a sentence below about what it might mean to accept them. For those you do control, can you think of one action you might take that would start making a positive difference, however small?

ER YOUR MIND, NOT
IZE THIS, AND YOU
MARCUS AURELIUS

Can you think of five changes you would like to make in your life? Whether they're big or small, try listing five goals below that you feel you'd like to achieve over the next year.

1

2

3

4

5

If you want to change something, one of the most important questions is not whether you eventually succeed, but how you get there – and deal with failures along the way.

Pick just one change from above, and work out how you can break down achieving it into a sequence of five smaller steps.

1

2

3

4

5

'Obstacles are those frightful things you see when you take your eyes off your goal.'

Henry Ford

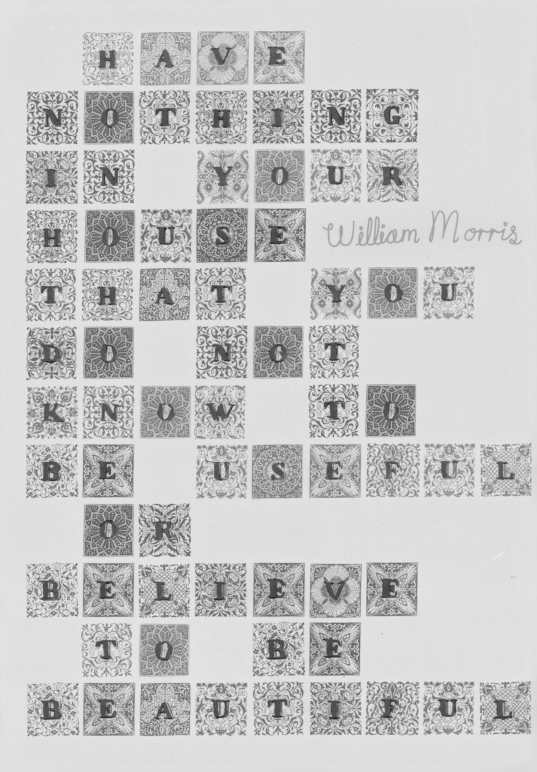

HAVE NOTHING IN YOUR HOUSE THAT YOU DO NOT KNOW TO BE USEFUL OR BELIEVE TO BE BEAUTIFUL

William Morris

Getting rid of clutter can be amazingly useful for clearing your mind. For each of the below, try getting rid of things you don't need or use any more; anything out-of-date or gathering dust. Donate excess to charity if you can – and record how many bags or boxes you've cleared for each one!

Desk and workspace

Bedroom and clothes

Letters, magazines and papers

Living and dining rooms

Kitchen, food and cupboards

Now that you've got rid of excess stuff, see if you can also de-clutter your time and attention: everything from computer files and excess appointments to email lists, notes and unwelcome social obligations. What would you be calmer and better off without? Record your successes and aims below.

Apps, digital files, programs

Subscriptions, email lists, groups, updates

Appointments, memberships, meetings

Social obligations, hobbies, habits

Redundant routine, daily nuisance

'Our anxiety does not empty tomorrow of its sorrows, but only empties today of its strengths.'

We sometimes talk about anxieties that 'keep us awake at night'. What worries rise to the surface of your mind when you relax? Try engaging with them by sitting quietly, clearing your thoughts, breathing comfortably – and then writing any insistent thoughts down below as they come into your mind.

Charles H. Spurgeon

What kind of thing have you written on the left? If some of them make you feel anxious, try actively shifting the way you think about them. Can you rephrase any anxious thoughts below in a way that is more emotionally neutral; that states facts rather than apportions blame; that puts them in context?

Giving up something for a length of time is among the most ancient of rituals, aimed at sharpening both inner and outer awareness – and not taking plenty or privilege for granted. Whether it's a food, drink, habit or comfort, self-denial is a discipline whose rewards can be enduring.

Choose something you're prepared to give up for a month – and keep a record of your commitment below. To track your progress, rate each day out of ten for difficulty, where one is the easiest and ten is the hardest. Stick with it, test your willpower – and observe how your sense of need shifts.

1   Today was a _____ out of ten
2   Today was a _____ out of ten
3   Today was a _____ out of ten
4   Today was a _____ out of ten
5   Today was a _____ out of ten
6   Today was a _____ out of ten
7   Today was a _____ out of ten
8   Today was a _____ out of ten
9   Today was a _____ out of ten
10 Today was a _____ out of ten
11 Today was a _____ out of ten
12 Today was a _____ out of ten
13 Today was a _____ out of ten
14 Today was a _____ out of ten
15 Today was a _____ out of ten
16 Today was a _____ out of ten

17 Today was a _____ out of ten
18 Today was a _____ out of ten
19 Today was a _____ out of ten
20 Today was a _____ out of ten
21 Today was a _____ out of ten
22 Today was a _____ out of ten
23 Today was a _____ out of ten
24 Today was a _____ out of ten
25 Today was a _____ out of ten
26 Today was a _____ out of ten
27 Today was a _____ out of ten
28 Today was a _____ out of ten
29 Today was a _____ out of ten
30 Today was a _____ out of ten
31 Today was a _____ out of ten

ABANDON OURSELVES?

How do you feel at the end? Was it harder or easier than you expected? What was best, worst and most surprising?

WHERE SHALL WE GO . . . ?'

ST GREGORY THE GREAT

'THE ENEMY IS FEAR. WE THINK IT IS HATE, BUT IT IS FEAR.'

Mahatma Gandhi

The fear of failure and disappointment can sabotage us before we even begin trying, but expressing our fears can help us gain perspective and negotiate rather than be paralysed. What are five things you want to do, and five worries in your way?

I would like   but I worry that

I would like   but I worry that

I would like   but I worry that

I would like   but I worry that

I would like   but I worry that

Try revisiting the five areas above – but this time listing not your worries, but a concrete first step you could take towards your goal. Ask yourself: why do I want to do this? And what will it mean to me? Don't fail before you've tried.

I want   and can start by

I want   and can start by

I want   and can start by

I want   and can start by

I want   and can start by

Do you have any time that's sacred in your day: clear time, uninterrupted, just for you? Try taking just fifteen minutes each day over the course of a week to sit, quiet and undistracted, in your own company – and record below one thought that came each day.

1

2

3

4

5

6

7

Safeguarding some time for yourself is important – but it's also important to invest time in other people who matter. Next week, try taking fifteen minutes each day to compose a short message to send to someone who matters to you.

1

2

3

4

5

6

7

'YOU MUST HAVE A ROOM OR A CERTAIN HOUR OR SO A DAY WHERE YOU DO NOT KNOW WHAT IS IN THE MORNING PAPER. A PLACE WHERE YOU CAN SIMPLY EXPERIENCE AND BRING FORTH WHAT YOU ARE AND WHAT YOU MIGHT BE.' JOSEPH CAMPBELL

'TO DO TWO THINGS AT ONCE IS TO DO NEITHER.

PUBLILIUS SYRUS

Learning to say 'no' can be at least as difficult as saying 'yes' to opportunities, yet they're closely related: you only have time to do what really matters if you're not spending that time elsewhere. Try listing five things you would love to have time to do but which, currently, you aren't able to say 'yes' to.

_____

_____

_____

_____

_____

If you want to say 'yes' to any of the aims you've listed, you may have to say 'no' not only to things you don't enjoy, but some you like. Imagine you had no choice but to create more free time in your life from somewhere. What would you give up? Think broadly enough and you may surprise yourself.

_____

_____

_____

_____

_____

'. . . the best way to give advice to your children

is to find out what they want

Giving useful criticism is a difficult skill to master.
Here are five suggestions:

1. Don't be personal: focus on actions, not the person.

2. Be specific: explain precisely what you're referring to.

3. Give reasons: explain the thinking behind your points.

4. Make suggestions for improvement: don't just be negative.

5. Make a plan for following up: it's all pointless if no changes
   are made.

Now try answering this. What are your strengths and
weaknesses when offering advice to others? What can
you try to do differently?

Harry Truman

and advise them to do it.'

Accepting and responding positively to criticism is just as hard. Here's some advice:

1. **Don't take it personally: stay calm and open-minded.**

2. **Really listen to what's being said: don't just deny it.**

3. **Ask questions: after you've listened, make sure you** clarify your understanding.

4. **Ensure you follow up: turn any insights into actions.**

5. **Know your critic's limitations: what do, and don't,** they really know about?

What are the most useful or insightful criticisms you have ever received? What actions might you take to respond to them?

What are the five things from this book that you have found most useful or interesting . . . ?

_____

_____

_____

_____

_____

. . . and which five have you enjoyed or liked least – or disagreed with. Why? What would you do differently?

_____

_____

_____

_____

_____

'I do not agree with what you have to say, but I'll defend to the death your right to say it.'

Voltaire*

* as summarized by Evelyn Beatrice Hall

I hope you've enjoyed reading and using this book, and that it's something you'll keep for many years.

It was certainly a pleasure to put it together – and a privilege to be so involved in creating a book that's also beautiful to look at, to hold, and to use.

Most of that beauty comes courtesy of Chris Bentham, the designer at Penguin who created every one of these pages. He's the one whose talent and graft gave everything life, and it has been humbling to see him turn my words again and again into something so bold and lovely.

I couldn't end a book like this without thanking Chris, or two other people without whom it wouldn't exist: my agent, Jon Elek, who looked at the enthusiastic mess of my initial proposal and thought it might work – and my editor at Penguin, Daniel Bunyard, who Jon rightly saw as the perfect man to make it happen, and who has been a miracle of support, enthusiasm and expertise.

Finally, I also need to thank *you*: for giving these words and pages your attention; for whatever time you have spent with this book; and for wherever you've allowed it to find a place in your life.

I would also love to know what you think about it. I will, let's be honest, be looking at comments and reviews and mentions and everything else I can't help but care about. But it would be lovely to hear from you in person, too.

So do feel free to send or share any thoughts – including your answers to the question on the previous page (about what you liked or found useful, and what you didn't) – in any way you fancy.

I'm on Twitter (@TomChatfield) and email (tom.chatfield@gmail.com) – or you can send a letter care of my publishers: Tom Chatfield c/o Penguin Publicity, 80 Strand, London WC2R 0RL. I'll aim to reply personally, though I can't promise to be speedy.

Thank you for reading, and writing, and thinking.